For my grandmother,
who always brought
apple pie
—H.M.Z.

Text copyright © 2005, 2023 by Harriet Ziefert
Illustrations copyright © 2005, 2023 by Amanda Haley
All rights reserved / CIP Data is available.
Published in the United States by
 Blue Apple Books
South Orange, New Jersey
www.blueapplebooks.com

41 USES
for a
GRANDMA

Harriet Ziefert
drawings by Amanda Haley

3. thermometer

4. lounge chair

5. dance instructor

6. page turner

7. hair braider

8. personal shopper

9. keeper of secrets

10. ballet barre

11. e-pal

12. play date

13. bearer of gifts

14. someone to love you
    when others may not

15. timekeeper

16. movie companion

17. coatroom

18. fan club

19.
mini kitchen

20.
jewelry box

21. baby-sitter

22. marathon runner

23. restaurant companion

24. pillow

25. valentine

26.
after-school

27.
yoga teacher

28. vacation destination

29. chef

30. towel rack

31. swim instructor

32. builder

33. history teacher

34.
monkey bars

35.
welcome mat

36. lifeguard

37. hiding place

38. decorator

39. pet sitter

40. ticket holder

41. friend

THE END

HARRIET ZIEFERT is the grandmother of William, Nathaniel, and Sylvie Anne, and the step-grandmother of Emma, Anna, Alexi, Saul, Jake, and Sam. She is the well-known author of more than two hundred books for children.

AMANDA HALEY collects antique toys, which often appear in her artwork. A graduate of *The School of the Art Institute of Chicago*, she now lives in Ohio with her husband, Brian, and their golden retriever, Sally.

www.ingramcontent.com/pod-product-compliance
Lightning Source LLC
LaVergne TN
LVHW070837080426
835510LV00026B/3424